YAKALOU MEDIA

15 Things You Should Let Go Before You Die

Why and What You Need To Do

First edition

This book was professionally typeset on Reedsy.
Find out more at reedsy.com

Contents

Disclaimer

This book is designed to provide information only. This information is provided and sold with the knowledge that the publisher and author do not offer any legal or other professional advice. In the case of a need for any such expertise, consult with the appropriate professional.

This book does not contain all the information available on the subject. This book has not been created to be specific to any individual's or organization's situation or needs. Every effort has been made to make this book as accurate as possible. However, there may be typographical and/or content errors. Therefore, this book should serve only as a general guide, not as the ultimate source of subject information.

This book contains information that might be dated and is intended only to educate and entertain. Regarding any loss or damage allegedly suffered or alleged to have occurred as a result of the information in this book, either directly or indirectly, the author and publisher shall have no liability or responsibility to any person or entity.

I

Let's Start Here

Introduction

Have you ever wondered what holds you back from living your best life? As we navigate through the hustle and bustle of daily life, we often accumulate emotional and mental baggage. This baggage, made up of regrets, fears, and grudges, weighs us down and prevents us from reaching our full potential. Imagine what it would be like to shed these burdens and experience life with a renewed sense of freedom and joy.

What if you could let go of the past and embrace the present fully? Many of us carry the weight of past mistakes, harbor resentments, and set unrealistic expectations for ourselves. These habits not only hinder our progress but also steal our peace of mind. By identifying and releasing these mental blocks, we can pave the way for a more fulfilling and meaningful life.

Have you considered the impact of your thoughts on your daily life? Negative self-talk and chronic worry can cloud our judgment and keep us from seeing the opportunities around us. The stories we tell ourselves shape our reality. So, what would happen if you changed the narrative and started speaking kindly to yourself?

Think about the relationships in your life. Are there any toxic connections that drain your energy and joy? Holding onto these relationships can prevent us from forming meaningful and supportive connections. Letting go of toxic relationships allows us to surround ourselves with positive influences and foster a nurturing environment.

What about the constant need for control and perfection? These desires can be exhausting and often leave us feeling unfulfilled. Accepting that not everything is within our control and embracing imperfection can lead to a more relaxed and happy life. Life is not about achieving perfection but about enjoying the journey and learning along the way.

Can you imagine a life without regrets? Letting go of regrets means forgiving yourself for past mistakes and understanding that those experiences shaped who you are today. By focusing on the present and future, we can create new, positive memories that overshadow any past regrets.

The aim of this book is to guide you through the process of letting go. Each chapter will explore a different aspect of life that you can release to lighten your load and enhance your well-being. By the end of this journey, you will have the tools to live more freely and authentically, without the burdens that have held you back.

Are you ready to embark on this journey of self-discovery and liberation? Let's dive in and explore the 15 things you should let go before you die, so you can live your life to the fullest.

The 7 Rules to Get the Most Out of This Book

Have you ever picked up a book, eager to learn and grow, only to find yourself drifting away after a few pages? Many of us have experienced this, and it's often because we haven't fully engaged with the material. To truly benefit from this book, you need a game plan. Here are the 7 rules to help you get the most out of this journey.

Rule 1: Approach with an Open Mind

Why is it important to start with an open mind? Because this book will challenge some of your deeply held beliefs and habits. To benefit fully, you need to be willing to consider new perspectives and try out new approaches. When you open your mind, you open yourself to growth and transformation.

Rule 2: Reflect and Journal

Have you ever tried writing down your thoughts and feelings? Journaling can be a powerful tool for reflection. As you read through each chapter, take a few moments to jot down your thoughts, reactions, and any insights you gain. This practice not only helps you remember what you've read but also deepens your understanding and personal connection to the material.

Rule 3: Take Your Time

Do you rush through books just to finish them? Resist that urge with this one. Take your time to absorb each chapter. Give yourself the space to think about how the concepts apply to your life. Reading slowly allows you to integrate the lessons and make lasting changes.

Rule 4: Discuss with Others

Have you ever learned something new and felt the urge to share it with someone? Talking about what you've read can reinforce your understanding and offer new insights. Find a friend, join a book club, or participate in online discussions about the book. These conversations can enrich your experience and provide different viewpoints.

Rule 5: Apply the Lessons

Reading without action is like dreaming without doing. Have you thought about how you can implement what you learn from this book into your daily life? Each chapter contains practical advice and exercises. Commit to trying them out. Start with small steps, and gradually incorporate these changes into your routine.

Rule 6: Revisit and Review

Do you remember everything you read the first time? Most of us don't. That's why it's beneficial to revisit and review the chapters periodically. Each time you go back, you might discover something you missed before. Repetition helps solidify your learning and keeps the lessons fresh in your mind.

Rule 7: Be Patient with Yourself

Change takes time. Have you ever felt frustrated when you don't see immediate results? Remember, personal growth is a journey, not a destination. Be kind and patient with yourself as you work through the book. Celebrate your progress, no matter how small, and understand that setbacks are part of the process.

By following these seven rules, you will set yourself up for a transformative experience. This book is designed to help you let go of what holds you back and embrace a more fulfilling life. Are you ready to start this journey? Let's dive in and make the most out of every page.

A Word of Warning Before We Start

Have you ever set out on a new journey, only to realize midway that it was much more challenging than you anticipated? As you prepare to embark on this transformative journey through the pages of this book, it's crucial to understand that letting go of deeply ingrained habits and beliefs is not an easy task. This chapter serves as a word of warning and preparation before we delve into the heart of the matter.

Why a Warning?

You might be wondering, why start with a warning? The answer is simple: to set realistic expectations. This book will ask you to confront aspects of yourself and your life that you may have avoided for years. It will require honesty, courage, and a willingness to change. Are you ready for this challenge? If you are, the rewards will be worth it.

Emotional Turbulence

Have you ever felt overwhelmed by your emotions? As you read and reflect on the topics in this book, you may experience a range of emotions—from sadness and anger to relief and joy. This is a normal part of the process. Embrace these feelings as signs of your progress. They are indicators that you are truly engaging with the material and making meaningful changes.

The Pain of Letting Go

Letting go can be painful. Have you ever had to part with something or someone important to you? Whether it's a relationship, a long-held belief, or a familiar habit, letting go often feels like a loss. Understand that this pain is temporary and a necessary step toward growth. By acknowledging this upfront, you prepare yourself to face and overcome these challenges.

Facing Resistance

Have you noticed how easy it is to fall back into old patterns? Change often triggers resistance. Your mind and body are accustomed to certain ways of thinking and behaving, and altering these patterns can be uncomfortable. Recognize that resistance is a natural response to change. Anticipate it, and instead of letting it derail your progress, use it as a signal to push forward.

Commitment to the Process

How committed are you to transforming your life? This book requires more than just passive reading. It demands active participation and a commitment to apply its lessons in your daily life. Set aside dedicated time to engage with the exercises and reflections. The more effort you put in, the more you will gain.

Support Systems

Have you thought about who can support you on this journey? Going through significant changes alone can be daunting. Reach out to friends, family, or support groups who can encourage you and hold you accountable. Sharing your journey with others can provide strength and perspective, making the process less isolating and more rewarding.

The Light at the End of the Tunnel

Despite the challenges, remember why you started this journey. Imagine a life where you are free from the burdens that have held you back. Picture yourself living with more joy, freedom, and fulfillment. This vision can be your guiding light when the path seems difficult.

A Final Thought

Before we dive into the specifics of what to let go of, take a moment to breathe deeply and center yourself. Acknowledge the bravery it takes to start this journey. Are you ready to transform your life and let go of what no longer serves you? If so, turn the page and let's begin this transformative adventure together.

With this word of warning, you are now better prepared for the challenges and rewards that lie ahead. Embrace the process, trust yourself, and know that each step brings you closer to a lighter, more fulfilling life. Let's embark on this journey of letting go, one chapter at a time.

Dive In Where It Feels Right

Have you ever felt overwhelmed by the prospect of reading a whole book from cover to cover? The good news is, you don't have to. This book is designed to be flexible and user-friendly, allowing you to skip around to the parts that resonate with you the most. Let's explore how you can get the most out of it, even if you don't read every single page.

Imagine you're sitting down after a long day, feeling particularly burdened by a specific issue. Maybe it's a lingering resentment or a constant fear that haunts you. Instead of starting at the beginning, you can flip directly to the chapter that addresses your current struggle. Each section of this book is crafted to stand alone, providing insights and practical advice that you can apply immediately.

Why is this approach beneficial? Life is unpredictable, and our needs change from day to day. Some days, you might be in the mood for deep reflection, while other days, you might just want a quick boost of inspiration. By allowing yourself to navigate the book based on your current emotional state, you make the process of letting go more manageable and personalized.

Consider the chapters as individual tools in a toolbox. Each one is designed to help you with a specific aspect of letting go. Whether you're dealing with perfectionism, toxic relationships, or the need for control, you can dive into the relevant chapter and find exactly what you need. This method keeps you engaged and prevents the feeling of being stuck or overwhelmed.

Isn't it liberating to know that you have the freedom to choose? As you explore the book, you'll find that some chapters speak to you more than others. That's perfectly okay. The goal is to make progress at your own pace and in your own way. Skipping around doesn't mean you're not committed; it means you're being thoughtful about what you need in the moment.

So, flip through the table of contents, scan the chapter titles, and let your intuition guide you. There's no wrong way to use this book. Trust yourself to know what you need, and allow this journey of letting go to unfold naturally, one page at a time.

II

The 15 Things You Should Let Go Before You Die

Chapter 1: Letting Go of Resentments

Understanding Resentments

Sarah had always been a cheerful and kind-hearted person. Her friends loved her optimism and infectious laughter. But over the years, something changed. Sarah started to carry a heaviness in her heart, a weight that seemed to grow day by day. It all began when her best friend, Emma, betrayed her trust by sharing a personal secret. Sarah felt hurt, betrayed, and angry. She tried to move on, but every time she saw Emma or heard her name, the old wound would reopen, and the bitterness would resurface. It affected Sarah's mood, her relationships, and even her health.

One day, during a casual conversation, a colleague mentioned how letting go of grudges had transformed her life. This piqued Sarah's interest. Could letting go of her resentment toward Emma bring back her peace and happiness? Determined to find out, Sarah began her journey toward forgiveness and emotional freedom.

What Are Resentments?

Resentment is a complex, multi-layered emotion that encompasses feelings of anger, hurt, and bitterness toward someone who has wronged you. It often arises from a sense of injustice or betrayal. Holding onto resentment can feel like carrying a heavy backpack filled with rocks. Each rock represents a grudge or a hurtful memory that weighs you down, making every step in life more difficult.

Have you ever noticed how thinking about a past wrong can instantly ruin your mood? That's the power of resentment. It keeps you trapped in a cycle of negativity, reliving the pain over and over. But why do we hold onto these feelings, even when they make us miserable?

The Impact of Resentments

Holding onto resentments can have serious consequences for your mental and physical health. Constantly dwelling on past hurts can lead to chronic stress, anxiety, and even depression. It can damage your relationships, as the bitterness you feel can spill over into your interactions with others. Over time, resentment can become a barrier to new experiences and personal growth, keeping you stuck in a loop of negativity.

Have you ever found it hard to enjoy a moment because a painful memory suddenly popped into your mind? That's resentment pulling you back into the past. But what if you could let go of that emotional baggage? What if you could free yourself from the grip of old grudges and move forward with a lighter heart?

Letting Go of Resentments

Letting go of resentment doesn't mean you are condoning the actions that hurt you. It simply means you are choosing to release the hold that these negative emotions have over your life. It's about reclaiming your power and emotional well-being.

1. **Acknowledge Your Feelings**: The first step to letting go is acknowledging that you feel resentful. Suppressing or denying your emotions only strengthens their grip. Take a moment to identify who or what you are holding a grudge against and why.

2. **Understand the Source**: Reflect on why the event or person affected you so deeply. Was it a betrayal of trust, a broken promise, or a harsh word? Understanding the source of your resentment can help you process your emotions more effectively.

3. **Empathize with the Other Person**: Try to see the situation from the other person's perspective. This doesn't mean excusing their behavior, but understanding their motives can sometimes make it easier to forgive.

4. **Decide to Forgive**: Forgiveness is a choice. It's a decision to let go of your anger and move on. This can be difficult, but remember, forgiveness is for your benefit, not necessarily for the person who hurt you.

5. **Seek Closure**: Sometimes, it helps to express your feelings to the person who hurt you. This can be done through a conversation, a letter, or even a personal journal entry. The goal is to release the pent-up emotions and find closure.

6. **Focus on the Present**: Living in the past prevents you from enjoying the present. Practice mindfulness and focus on the positive aspects of your life. Engage in activities that bring you joy and fulfillment.

Why Let Go of Resentments?

Letting go of resentment can free up your emotional space, allowing you to feel lighter, happier, and more at peace. It can improve your relationships, reduce stress, and enhance your overall well-being. Imagine walking through life without that heavy backpack of grudges. How much easier and more enjoyable would each step be?

Practical Steps for Change

To truly let go of resentment, it takes more than just understanding the process. It requires consistent effort and self-reflection. Here are some practical steps you can take:

1. **Daily Reflection**: Spend a few minutes each day reflecting on your feelings. Are there any new resentments forming? Address them before they grow.
2. **Gratitude Journal**: Start a gratitude journal to shift your focus from what has hurt you to what blesses you. Each day, write down three things you are grateful for.
3. **Mindfulness Meditation**: Practice mindfulness meditation to stay present and avoid getting lost in past grievances.
4. **Positive Affirmations**: Use positive affirmations to reinforce your decision to let go of resentment. Remind yourself daily that you are choosing peace over bitterness.
5. **Seek Professional Help**: If you find it particularly challenging to let go of resentment, consider seeking help from a therapist or counselor. They can provide tools and strategies tailored to your needs.

Questions for Reflection

1. Who in your life have you been holding a grudge against, and why?
2. How has holding onto this resentment affected your mental and physical health?

18

3. What steps can you take to understand the other person's perspective?
4. How would letting go of this resentment change your daily life?
5. What positive experiences or relationships have you missed out on because of your grudges?

Practical Exercise

Write a letter to the person you hold resentment toward. In this letter, express your feelings honestly but respectfully. You don't need to send this letter. The goal is to release your emotions and find closure within yourself. After writing the letter, reflect on how you feel and what steps you can take next to move forward.

Letting go of resentment is not easy, but it's one of the most liberating things you can do for yourself. By choosing to release old grudges, you open up space for joy, peace, and new positive experiences in your life. Remember, you deserve to live free from the weight of past hurts.

Chapter 2: Letting Go of Fear of Failure

Release the Fear That Prevents You from Trying New Things or Taking Risks

Jack had always dreamed of starting his own business. He had a brilliant idea for a unique café that combined a cozy atmosphere with an array of board games for patrons to enjoy. Despite his passion and detailed plans, Jack never took the first step. Why? He was paralyzed by the fear of failure. The "what ifs" haunted him day and night. What if the business fails? What if no one likes the concept? What if he loses all his savings? These fears kept Jack stuck in his safe but unfulfilling job, year after year.

One day, Jack met an old friend, Laura, who had recently launched her own startup. Laura shared her own fears and failures, but more importantly, she shared how each failure had taught her valuable lessons and eventually led to her success. Inspired by Laura's story, Jack decided it was time to confront his fear of failure head-on and give his dream a real chance.

Understanding the Fear of Failure

The fear of failure is a deeply ingrained fear that can prevent us from taking risks, trying new things, and ultimately pursuing our dreams. It is the fear of making mistakes, looking foolish, or not living up to our own or others' expectations. This fear can be crippling, creating a mental barrier that holds us back from potential opportunities and growth.

Have you ever avoided trying something new because you were afraid you might fail? This fear often whispers in our ears, telling us that it's better to stay in our comfort zone where it's safe. But what if we never step out of that zone? What dreams and opportunities are we missing out on?

The Impact of Fear of Failure

The impact of the fear of failure can be profound. It can stifle creativity, limit personal and professional growth, and lead to a life filled with regret and what-ifs. When we let fear dictate our actions, we miss out on the richness of experiences and the satisfaction of achieving our goals.

Think about a time when you let fear stop you from pursuing something you really wanted. How did it make you feel? Chances are, you felt a mix of relief and disappointment. Relief because you avoided the risk, but disappointment because you didn't give yourself a chance to succeed. Imagine if you could turn that disappointment into a triumph. How would your life change?

Overcoming the Fear of Failure

Overcoming the fear of failure is not about eliminating the fear completely; it's about learning to manage and move past it. Here are some strategies to help you face and conquer this fear:

1. **Reframe Your Perspective**: Instead of viewing failure as a negative outcome, see it as a learning opportunity. Each failure brings valuable lessons that can lead you closer to success. Ask yourself, "What can I learn from this

experience?"

2. **Set Realistic Goals**: Break your larger goals into smaller, manageable steps. Achieving these smaller milestones can build your confidence and reduce the fear of failing at the larger task.

3. **Visualize Success**: Spend time each day visualizing your success. Picture yourself achieving your goals and enjoying the fruits of your efforts. This positive visualization can boost your motivation and reduce your fear.

4. **Accept Imperfection**: Understand that perfection is unattainable. Allow yourself to make mistakes and learn from them. Embrace your imperfections as part of your growth journey.

5. **Build a Support System**: Surround yourself with supportive people who encourage and believe in you. Share your fears with them and seek their advice and encouragement.

6. **Take Action**: The best way to overcome fear is to take action. Start with small steps and gradually take on bigger challenges. Each step you take will build your courage and reduce your fear.

Why Let Go of Fear of Failure?

Letting go of the fear of failure opens up a world of possibilities. It allows you to pursue your dreams, take risks, and explore new opportunities without being held back by self-doubt. By facing your fear, you gain confidence, resilience, and a sense of accomplishment. Imagine the freedom of living a life where fear doesn't dictate your choices. What incredible things could you achieve?

Practical Steps for Change

To effectively let go of your fear of failure, consistent practice and self-reflection are key. Here are some practical steps to guide you:

1. **Daily Affirmations**: Use daily affirmations to reinforce your belief in your abilities. Statements like "I am capable of achieving my goals" can help build your confidence.
2. **Journaling**: Keep a journal to document your fears and the steps you are taking to overcome them. Reflect on your progress and celebrate your successes, no matter how small.
3. **Mindfulness Practice**: Practice mindfulness to stay present and reduce anxiety about future failures. Mindfulness can help you stay focused on the task at hand rather than getting lost in what-ifs.
4. **Seek Mentorship**: Find a mentor who has overcome similar fears and can provide guidance and support. Learning from someone who has faced and conquered their fears can be incredibly motivating.
5. **Embrace Challenges**: Actively seek out and embrace challenges that push you out of your comfort zone. The more you face your fears, the less power they have over you.

Questions for Reflection

1. What is one thing you have always wanted to try but have been too afraid to pursue?
2. How has the fear of failure held you back in your personal or professional life?
3. What steps can you take today to start overcoming your fear of failure?

4. How would your life change if you no longer let fear control your decisions?
5. Who can you turn to for support and encouragement as you face your fears?

Practical Exercise

Choose one fear of failure that has been holding you back. Write down three small steps you can take to confront this fear. For each step, note what you might learn from the experience, regardless of the outcome. Over the next week, commit to taking these steps and reflect on your progress. How does taking action impact your fear and your confidence?

Facing the fear of failure is a courageous step toward living a fuller, more authentic life. By choosing to confront your fears, you empower yourself to grow, learn, and achieve your true potential. Remember, the path to success is often paved with failures, each one bringing you closer to your dreams. You have the strength to overcome your fears and embrace the opportunities that lie ahead.

Chapter 3: Letting Go of Unrealistic Expectations

Stop Setting Standards That Are Too High for Yourself or Others

Emma had always been a perfectionist. From a young age, she excelled in school, sports, and music, driven by the high standards she set for herself. As she grew older, these expectations extended to her career, relationships, and personal achievements. Emma believed that if she worked hard enough, she could achieve perfection in every aspect of her life. But the constant pressure to meet these impossible standards took a toll on her mental and physical health. She felt exhausted, stressed, and never truly satisfied with her accomplishments.

One day, Emma's best friend, Lily, shared an insight that changed her perspective. "Perfection doesn't exist, Emma. You're already amazing as you are." This simple statement sparked a realization in Emma. She began to question her unrealistic expectations and sought ways to adjust them for a healthier, more fulfilling life.

What Are Unrealistic Expectations?

Unrealistic expectations are standards or goals that are impossible or extremely difficult to achieve. They can stem from societal pressures, personal insecurities, or a desire for control and perfection. These expectations often lead to disappointment, frustration, and a sense of failure because they are unattainable.

Have you ever set a goal that seemed reasonable at the time but later felt overwhelming? Perhaps you wanted to lose a significant amount of weight in a short period of time, excel in a new hobby instantly, or expect your partner to understand your needs without communication. These are all examples of unrealistic expectations. But why do we set such high standards for ourselves and others?

The Impact of Unrealistic Expectations

Unrealistic expectations can negatively impact our mental health and relationships. When we set the bar too high, we set ourselves up for failure. This can lead to feelings of inadequacy, low self-esteem, and chronic stress. Moreover, imposing unrealistic expectations on others can strain relationships, as it creates pressure and potential conflict.

Think about a time when you set unrealistic expectations for yourself or someone else. How did it feel when those expectations weren't met? The likely result was frustration, disappointment, or even resentment. But what if we could learn to set more realistic, achievable goals? How would that change our daily lives and interactions with others?

Setting Realistic Goals

Adjusting your expectations involves setting realistic, achievable goals that allow for flexibility and growth. Here are some strategies to help you set more realistic expectations:

1. **Assess Your Current Situation**: Take a realistic look at your

current abilities, resources, and limitations. Understand where you are starting from and what is feasible given your circumstances.

2. **Break Down Goals**: Instead of setting a large, overwhelming goal, break it down into smaller, manageable steps. Achieving these smaller milestones can build your confidence and keep you motivated.

3. **Allow for Flexibility**: Life is unpredictable, and circumstances can change. Allow yourself to adjust your goals as needed without feeling like you have failed.

4. **Focus on Progress, Not Perfection**: Celebrate your progress and small victories along the way. Understand that perfection is not the goal; continuous improvement is.

5. **Seek Feedback and Support**: Talk to trusted friends, family, or mentors about your goals. They can provide valuable feedback and support to help you stay on track and adjust your expectations as needed.

Why Let Go of Unrealistic Expectations?

Letting go of unrealistic expectations can lead to greater happiness, reduced stress, and improved relationships. When we set realistic goals, we give ourselves permission to be human and make mistakes. This shift in mindset can lead to a more balanced, fulfilling life.

Imagine how freeing it would be to live without the constant pressure of unrealistic standards. What would you achieve if you approached your goals with compassion and flexibility?

Practical Steps for Change

To effectively let go of unrealistic expectations, consistent effort and self-reflection are essential. Here are some practical steps to guide you:

1. **Daily Reflection**: Spend a few minutes each day reflecting on your goals and expectations. Are they realistic and achievable given your current situation?
2. **Adjust Goals Regularly**: Revisit your goals periodically and adjust them as needed. Life changes, and so should your expectations.
3. **Celebrate Small Wins**: Take time to celebrate your progress, no matter how small. Recognize that each step forward is an achievement.
4. **Practice Self-Compassion**: Be kind to yourself when things don't go as planned. Understand that setbacks are a natural part of the journey.
5. **Seek Professional Guidance**: If you find it difficult to set realistic goals, consider seeking help from a coach or therapist. They can provide tools and strategies to help you set and achieve realistic expectations.

Questions for Reflection

1. What is one unrealistic expectation you have set for yourself or others recently?
2. How has holding onto this expectation affected your well-being or relationships?
3. What steps can you take to adjust this expectation to be more realistic?
4. How would your life change if you embraced more flexible and achievable goals?
5. Who can you turn to for support and feedback as you adjust

your expectations?

Practical Exercise

Choose one unrealistic expectation you have been holding onto. Write down why it is unrealistic and how it has impacted you. Then, reframe this expectation into a more realistic goal. For example, if you expect to lose 20 pounds in one month, adjust it to a goal of losing 1-2 pounds per week. Track your progress over the next month and reflect on how this new, realistic goal makes you feel compared to the previous one.

Letting go of unrealistic expectations is a crucial step towards living a balanced and fulfilling life. By setting realistic goals, you give yourself the grace to grow, learn, and succeed at your own pace. Remember, life is a journey, and every small step forward is a victory worth celebrating.

Chapter 4: Letting Go of Past Mistakes

Forgive Yourself for Past Errors and Learn from Them Without Letting Them Define You

Julia had always been a conscientious person, careful with her decisions and actions. But a few years ago, she made a significant mistake at work that cost her company a valuable client. The mistake haunted her, replaying in her mind every time she faced a new challenge. She constantly second-guessed herself, fearing she would make another error. This fear and regret affected her confidence and her ability to perform well in her job.

One day, during a conversation with her mentor, Julia shared her ongoing guilt. Her mentor listened patiently and then said, "Julia, we all make mistakes. What matters is how we learn from them and move forward. Forgive yourself and use this experience to grow." This advice was a turning point for Julia. She began to understand that her past mistake didn't define her; it was a stepping stone to becoming wiser and more resilient.

Why Past Mistakes Haunt Us

Past mistakes often linger in our minds, creating feelings of guilt and regret. These emotions can be powerful, causing us to relive our errors repeatedly. But why do we hold onto these feelings so tightly?

Guilt is a natural response when we believe we have violated our own moral standards or caused harm to others. Regret, on the other hand, stems from the desire to change the past. Together, these emotions can create a mental loop where we constantly replay our mistakes, wishing we could undo them.

Have you ever found yourself thinking, "If only I had done things differently"? This thought pattern keeps us stuck in the past, unable to move forward. But what if we could break free from this cycle? What if we could forgive ourselves and use our past mistakes as a foundation for growth?

The Impact of Guilt and Regret

Living with unresolved guilt and regret can have a detrimental impact on our mental and physical well-being. These emotions can lead to chronic stress, anxiety, and even depression. They can erode our self-esteem, making us feel unworthy or incapable of success.

Think about a time when you were overwhelmed by guilt or regret. How did it affect your daily life and interactions with others? Chances are, it made you less confident, more anxious, and perhaps even withdrawn. But imagine if you could let go of these burdens. How much lighter and more positive would your life become?

Forgiveness and Learning

Forgiving yourself for past mistakes is essential for personal growth and emotional well-being. Here are some techniques to help you forgive yourself and learn from your mistakes:

1. **Acknowledge Your Mistakes**: The first step to forgiveness

is acknowledging your mistakes. Accept responsibility for your actions without making excuses. This acknowledgment is crucial for moving forward.

2. **Understand the Root Cause**: Reflect on why you made the mistake. Were there external pressures, lack of knowledge, or other factors that influenced your decision? Understanding the root cause can help you avoid similar mistakes in the future.

3. **Practice Self-Compassion**: Treat yourself with the same kindness and understanding you would offer a friend. Recognize that making mistakes is part of being human. Be gentle with yourself as you navigate your emotions.

4. **Learn from the Experience**: Identify the lessons you can learn from your mistake. How can this experience make you wiser and more resilient? Use this knowledge to make better decisions moving forward.

5. **Release the Guilt**: Holding onto guilt serves no purpose other than to keep you stuck in the past. Consciously decide to release the guilt. Remind yourself that you are worthy of forgiveness and that everyone makes mistakes.

6. **Seek Closure**: If possible, take steps to make amends or rectify the situation. This can help you find closure and move on. If direct action is not possible, consider symbolic acts like writing a letter to yourself or engaging in a ritual to signify letting go.

Why Let Go of Past Mistakes?

Letting go of past mistakes allows you to reclaim your confidence and emotional freedom. It frees you from the mental burden of guilt and regret, enabling you to focus on the present and future. By forgiving yourself, you open up space for new opportunities, growth, and happiness.

Imagine how liberating it would be to live without the shadow of past mistakes hanging over you. What new paths could you explore if you weren't held back by regret?

Practical Steps for Change

To effectively let go of past mistakes, consistent effort and self-reflection are essential. Here are some practical steps to guide you:

1. **Daily Affirmations**: Use daily affirmations to reinforce your self-worth and forgiveness. Statements like "I forgive myself and embrace my growth" can help shift your mindset.
2. **Journaling**: Keep a journal to document your feelings and progress. Write about your mistakes, what you've learned, and how you're moving forward. Reflecting on your journey can provide clarity and motivation.
3. **Mindfulness Practice**: Practice mindfulness to stay present and avoid dwelling on past mistakes. Mindfulness techniques, such as deep breathing and meditation, can help you focus on the here and now.
4. **Seek Support**: Talk to a trusted friend, family member, or therapist about your feelings. Sharing your experiences can provide relief and perspective.
5. **Engage in Positive Activities**: Engage in activities that bring you joy and fulfillment. This can help you build positive experiences that counterbalance the negative feelings associated with past mistakes.

Questions for Reflection

1. What is one past mistake that you find difficult to let go of, and why?
2. How has holding onto this mistake affected your self-esteem and daily life?
3. What lessons have you learned from this experience that can help you in the future?
4. How can you practice self-compassion when reflecting on your past mistakes?
5. What steps can you take today to begin forgiving yourself and moving forward?

Practical Exercise

Write a letter to yourself about a past mistake you've been holding onto. In this letter, acknowledge the mistake, express your feelings about it, and outline what you've learned from the experience. End the letter with words of forgiveness and encouragement. After writing the letter, read it aloud to yourself and then store it in a safe place or symbolically let it go by tearing it up or burning it. Reflect on how this exercise makes you feel and what steps you can take next to continue your journey of self-forgiveness.

Letting go of past mistakes is a crucial step towards self-acceptance and personal growth. By forgiving yourself, you free up mental and emotional space for new experiences and opportunities. Remember, your mistakes do not define you— they are simply stepping stones on your journey to becoming a stronger, wiser person. You have the power to move forward and create a fulfilling life free from the shadows of the past.

Chapter 5: Letting Go of the Need for Control

Accept That Some Situations Are Beyond Your Control and Focus on What You Can Influence

Mark was always the planner in his group of friends. He meticulously organized every detail of trips, dinners, and even casual get-togethers. At work, his desk was filled with to-do lists and schedules. Mark believed that if he could control every aspect of his life, he could avoid any unexpected problems. But despite his efforts, things didn't always go as planned. Flights got delayed, meetings ran over time, and sometimes people simply didn't follow through. Each disruption caused Mark immense stress and frustration. He found himself constantly on edge, trying to maintain control over everything and everyone.

One evening, after a particularly stressful day where nothing went as planned, Mark's friend Lisa shared a piece of wisdom. "You can't control everything, Mark. Sometimes, you just have to go with the flow." This simple piece of advice struck a chord with him. Mark realized that his need for control was causing more harm than good. It was time to let go and focus on what he could influence rather than trying to control every outcome.

Control Issues

The need for control stems from a desire to manage uncertainty and prevent unwanted outcomes. While some level of control is necessary and beneficial, an excessive need for control can lead to significant stress and anxiety. Trying to micromanage every detail of life is exhausting and often futile because many factors are beyond our control.

Have you ever found yourself getting upset because things didn't go exactly as you planned? This reaction is common among those who struggle with control issues. But what if we could learn to accept the unpredictability of life and focus on what we can actually influence? How much stress could we alleviate?

How Trying to Control Everything Creates Stress

When we try to control every aspect of our lives, we set ourselves up for constant disappointment. Life is inherently unpredictable, and unforeseen events are bound to happen. By clinging to the need for control, we create a cycle of stress and frustration. Each unexpected event becomes a source of anxiety, and our inability to manage these events can lead to feelings of helplessness and inadequacy.

Think about a recent situation where things didn't go as you expected. How did it make you feel? Were you frustrated, anxious, or upset? Imagine if you had approached that situation with a mindset of acceptance and adaptability. How might your experience have been different?

Acceptance and Adaptability

Learning to accept what you cannot change and adapting to new circumstances is crucial for reducing stress and living a more fulfilling life. Here are some strategies to help you let go of the need for control:

1. **Identify What You Can and Cannot Control**: Make a list of things you can control (like your actions and responses) and things you cannot control (like other people's actions and unforeseen events). Focus your energy on the former and let go of the latter.
2. **Practice Mindfulness**: Mindfulness helps you stay present and reduces anxiety about the future. By focusing on the here and now, you can better manage your reactions to unexpected events.
3. **Embrace Flexibility**: Adopt a flexible mindset that allows you to adapt to changes and challenges. This doesn't mean giving up on planning, but rather being open to adjusting your plans as needed.
4. **Develop Coping Strategies**: Equip yourself with coping mechanisms for dealing with stress, such as deep breathing, meditation, or physical activity. These techniques can help you stay calm and composed in the face of uncertainty.
5. **Seek Support**: Talk to friends, family, or a therapist about your struggles with control. Sometimes, sharing your feelings and getting an outside perspective can provide relief and new insights.

Why Let Go of the Need for Control?

Letting go of the need for control can lead to a more peaceful and balanced life. By accepting that some situations are beyond your control, you can reduce stress and anxiety. Focusing on what you can influence allows you to direct your energy more productively and enjoy the present moment.

Imagine how freeing it would be to stop worrying about things you cannot change. What new opportunities and experiences could you embrace if you let go of the need for control?

Practical Steps for Change

To effectively let go of the need for control, consistent effort and self-reflection are essential. Here are some practical steps to guide you:

1. **Daily Reflection**: Spend a few minutes each day reflecting on situations where you felt the need to control. How did it make you feel, and what could you have done differently?
2. **Mindfulness Practice**: Incorporate mindfulness exercises into your daily routine to help you stay present and reduce anxiety about the future.
3. **Adaptability Challenges**: Challenge yourself to adapt to un-expected changes without stress. Start with small changes and gradually tackle larger ones.
4. **Positive Affirmations**: Use positive affirmations to rein-force your acceptance of unpredictability. Statements like "I embrace change and adapt easily" can help shift your mindset.
5. **Support Network**: Build a support network of people who understand your struggles and can offer encouragement and advice.

Questions for Reflection

1. What are some things in your life that you try to control but cannot?
2. How does the need for control affect your stress levels and relationships?

3. What strategies can you use to become more adaptable to unexpected changes?
4. How would your life change if you focused only on what you could influence?
5. Who can you talk to for support and guidance as you work on letting go of control?

Practical Exercise

Create a "Circle of Control" diagram. Draw two circles on a piece of paper, one inside the other. In the inner circle, write down the things you can control, such as your actions, thoughts, and responses. In the outer circle, write down the things you cannot control, like other people's actions, the weather, or unexpected events. Reflect on this diagram daily and remind yourself to focus on the inner circle. Over time, practice shifting your energy and attention to what you can control and letting go of the rest.

Letting go of the need for control is a journey toward greater peace and resilience. By accepting the unpredictability of life and focusing on what you can influence, you can reduce stress and open yourself up to new possibilities. Remember, true strength lies not in controlling every aspect of life but in adapting gracefully to its ever-changing nature. You have the power to embrace this change and live a more balanced, fulfilling life.

Chapter 6: Letting Go of Materialism

Embrace a Simpler Life and Focus on Experiences

Samantha always loved shopping. Every weekend, she would visit the mall, drawn by the latest fashion trends and gadgets. Her home was filled with clothes, accessories, and electronics, most of which she rarely used. She believed that owning more would make her happier. But despite her overflowing wardrobe and latest technology, Samantha often felt unfulfilled and anxious about her mounting credit card debt.

One day, while chatting with her friend Rachel, who had recently downsized her belongings and embraced minimalism, Samantha noticed a stark difference in their stress levels. Rachel seemed happier and more content, attributing her peace to letting go of unnecessary possessions. Inspired by Rachel's experience, Samantha decided it was time to reassess her relationship with material things.

Materialism Explained

Materialism is the belief that happiness and fulfillment come from acquiring possessions. It's a mindset heavily influenced by modern consumer culture, which constantly bombards us with advertisements promising that the next purchase will bring us joy. However, this pursuit of material goods often leads to temporary satisfaction followed by a desire for more, creating a never-ending cycle.

Have you ever felt a rush of excitement when buying something new, only to find that the feeling fades quickly? This is the false promise of materialism. It tricks us into believing that possessions can fill emotional voids and bring lasting happiness. But why does materialism fall short of fulfilling our deeper needs?

The False Promise of Happiness Through Possessions

Material possessions can provide temporary pleasure and convenience, but they rarely lead to lasting happiness. Studies have shown that experiences, rather than things, contribute more significantly to our overall well-being. Experiences create memories, foster connections with others, and contribute to our personal growth.

Think about a time when you bought something you really wanted. How long did the excitement last? Now compare that to a memorable experience, like a trip or a special event with loved ones. Which one brings a smile to your face now? Chances are, the experience holds more lasting value.

Embracing Minimalism

Minimalism is a lifestyle that encourages living with less and focusing on what truly matters. It's about decluttering your life, not just physically but also mentally and emotionally, to create space for meaningful experiences and relationships. Here are some tips for embracing minimalism:

1. **Declutter Your Space**: Start by going through your belongings and removing items that no longer serve a purpose

or bring you joy. Donate, sell, or recycle these items. This process can be liberating and help you appreciate what you truly need.

2. **Prioritize Experiences Over Things**: Shift your focus from acquiring possessions to creating experiences. Plan trips, attend events, or spend quality time with loved ones. These moments are more likely to bring lasting happiness than material goods.

3. **Simplify Your Purchases**: Before buying something new, ask yourself if it's truly necessary and if it will add value to your life. This can help you make more mindful purchasing decisions.

4. **Create a Capsule Wardrobe**: Limit your wardrobe to a select number of versatile pieces that you love and wear regularly. This reduces decision fatigue and keeps your closet organized.

5. **Focus on Quality Over Quantity**: Invest in high-quality items that are durable and timeless rather than accumulating numerous low-quality goods. This approach can save you money in the long run and reduce waste.

6. **Practice Gratitude**: Regularly take time to appreciate what you already have. Gratitude can shift your mindset from wanting more to being content with less.

Why Let Go of Materialism?

Letting go of materialism can lead to a more fulfilling and stress-free life. By reducing your reliance on possessions for happiness, you can focus on experiences that enrich your life and build meaningful connections. Embracing minimalism allows you to prioritize what truly matters and find contentment in simplicity.

Imagine a life where you are not constantly chasing the next purchase. How much more time and energy could you devote to the people and activities that bring you genuine joy?

Practical Steps for Change

To effectively let go of materialism, consistent effort and self-reflection are essential. Here are some practical steps to guide you:

1. **Daily Reflection**: Spend a few minutes each day reflecting on what truly brings you happiness. Is it possessions or experiences? Adjust your focus accordingly.
2. **Mindful Consumption**: Practice mindful consumption by being aware of your buying habits and the motivations behind them. Aim to make purchases that align with your values and needs.
3. **Experience Journal**: Keep a journal to document memorable experiences and the joy they bring. Reflecting on these entries can reinforce the value of experiences over possessions.
4. **Gratitude Practice**: Incorporate a gratitude practice into your daily routine. List three things you are grateful for each day to cultivate contentment.
5. **Community Support**: Join a community or online group of like-minded individuals who embrace minimalism. Sharing your journey with others can provide support and inspiration.

Questions for Reflection

1. What possessions do you have that bring you the least

amount of joy or usefulness?

2. How has the pursuit of material goods impacted your happiness and stress levels?

3. What experiences have brought you lasting happiness compared to material possessions?

4. How can you start prioritizing experiences over things in your daily life?

5. Who can you share your journey toward minimalism with for support and encouragement?

Practical Exercise

Choose one area of your home to declutter, such as your closet, kitchen, or living room. Set aside time to go through each item in this space and ask yourself if it truly adds value to your life. If it doesn't, consider donating, selling, or recycling it. As you clear the clutter, reflect on how this process makes you feel and how it impacts your mindset. Repeat this exercise for other areas of your home over time.

Letting go of materialism and embracing minimalism can lead to a richer, more meaningful life. By focusing on experiences and relationships rather than possessions, you can create lasting happiness and reduce stress. Remember, the most valuable things in life are not things—they are the moments, connections, and memories that fill our hearts and minds. You have the power to choose a simpler, more fulfilling path.

Chapter 7: Letting Go of Procrastination

Overcome Delaying Tasks and Build Proactive Habits

John was known for his brilliant ideas and creative mind. He had plans to write a novel, start a blog, and even learn a new language. However, despite his grand ambitions, John struggled with one major obstacle: procrastination. Every time he sat down to work on his goals, he found himself distracted by social media, household chores, or the latest Netflix series. Weeks turned into months, and John realized he hadn't made any significant progress. His dreams remained unfulfilled, buried under a mountain of excuses and delayed tasks.

One day, after yet another unproductive day, John decided enough was enough. He sought advice from a friend who was exceptionally productive. His friend explained how overcoming procrastination had transformed his life and shared strategies that had worked for him. Inspired and determined, John decided to tackle his procrastination head-on.

Procrastination Pitfalls

Procrastination is the act of delaying tasks that need to be done, often until the last minute or even indefinitely. While it might provide temporary relief or enjoyment, procrastination can significantly hinder your progress and overall well-being.

It can lead to missed opportunities, increased stress, and a constant sense of unaccomplishment.

Have you ever put off a task, thinking you had plenty of time, only to feel overwhelmed as the deadline approached? This is a common consequence of procrastination. But what if you could break this cycle and become more proactive? How much more could you achieve?

How Delaying Tasks Harms Your Progress

When you procrastinate, you create a cycle of stress and inefficiency. Tasks pile up, deadlines become tighter, and the quality of your work often suffers. Procrastination can also harm your self-esteem and confidence, as you constantly feel like you're falling behind or failing to meet your goals.

Think about a project or goal you've been putting off. How does it make you feel every time you think about it? Likely, it brings a sense of dread or guilt. Now imagine the relief and satisfaction you'd feel if you tackled it head-on and made steady progress. How would that change your outlook and productivity?

Building Proactive Habits

Overcoming procrastination involves developing proactive habits that keep you motivated and on track. Here are some strategies to help you break free from procrastination and build a more productive routine:

1. **Set Clear Goals**: Define what you want to achieve with specific, measurable, and realistic goals. Break larger tasks into smaller, manageable steps to make them less daunting.

2. **Create a Schedule**: Plan your day with a detailed schedule that includes time blocks for work, breaks, and personal activities. Having a structured plan can help you stay focused and avoid distractions.

3. **Prioritize Tasks**: Use a prioritization system, like the Eisenhower Matrix, to determine which tasks are urgent and important. Focus on completing high-priority tasks first to ensure you make progress on your most critical goals.

4. **Eliminate Distractions**: Identify and remove distractions from your work environment. This could mean turning off notifications, setting specific times for checking emails, or creating a dedicated workspace.

5. **Use Productivity Tools**: Utilize tools and apps designed to boost productivity, such as task managers, timers, and habit trackers. These can help you stay organized and accountable.

6. **Practice Self-Discipline**: Develop self-discipline by setting boundaries and sticking to your commitments. Reward yourself for completing tasks and hold yourself accountable for delays.

7. **Seek Accountability**: Share your goals with a friend or mentor who can provide support and hold you accountable. Regular check-ins can motivate you to stay on track.

Why Let Go of Procrastination?

Letting go of procrastination can lead to a more fulfilling and productive life. By tackling tasks promptly and consistently, you can reduce stress, achieve your goals, and build confidence in your abilities. Overcoming procrastination allows you to take control of your time and make the most of every opportunity.

Imagine the satisfaction of checking off tasks from your to-do list and seeing tangible progress toward your goals. How much more could you accomplish if you no longer let procrastination hold you back?

Practical Steps for Change

To effectively overcome procrastination, consistent effort and self-reflection are essential. Here are some practical steps to guide you:

1. **Daily Reflection**: Spend a few minutes each day reflecting on your productivity. Identify what tasks you procrastinated on and why. Use this insight to adjust your approach the next day.

2. **Time Blocking**: Implement time blocking in your daily schedule. Dedicate specific time slots to different tasks and stick to them. This can help create a sense of urgency and structure.

3. **Set Daily Goals**: At the start of each day, set three main goals you want to achieve. Focus on completing these tasks to build momentum and a sense of accomplishment.

4. **Mindfulness Practice**: Practice mindfulness to stay present and reduce anxiety about future tasks. Techniques like deep breathing and meditation can help you stay focused and calm.

5. **Reward System**: Create a reward system for yourself. Set small rewards for completing tasks and larger rewards for achieving major milestones. This can provide motivation and make the process more enjoyable.

Questions for Reflection

48

1. What tasks or goals have you been procrastinating on, and why?
2. How has procrastination affected your progress and well-being?
3. What strategies can you implement to reduce distractions and stay focused?
4. How would overcoming procrastination change your daily life and overall productivity?
5. Who can you share your goals with to help hold you accountable?

Practical Exercise

Choose one task you have been procrastinating on. Break it down into three smaller steps and set a deadline for each step. Schedule these steps into your daily planner or calendar. As you complete each step, reflect on how it makes you feel and any challenges you faced. Use this exercise to build momentum and confidence in tackling larger tasks.

Letting go of procrastination is a journey toward greater productivity and fulfillment. By developing proactive habits and staying motivated, you can achieve your goals and reduce stress. Remember, every small step forward is progress. You have the power to overcome procrastination and create a more productive, satisfying life.

Chapter 8: Letting Go of Negative Self-Talk

Replace Critical Inner Dialogue with Positive Affirmations

Emma always dreamed of starting her own business. She had a brilliant idea for a boutique coffee shop that would serve artisanal blends in a cozy, inviting space. However, every time she considered taking the first step, a harsh voice in her head would whisper, "You're not good enough. What if you fail?" This negative self-talk paralyzed her, preventing her from pursuing her dreams.

One day, after a particularly discouraging bout of self-doubt, Emma confided in her friend Sarah, who had recently opened her own successful bakery. Sarah listened empathetically and then shared a secret. "I used to struggle with the same thoughts," she said, "but I learned to replace them with positive affirmations. It changed everything." Inspired by Sarah's story, Emma decided to tackle her negative self-talk and replace it with a more supportive inner dialogue.

Harmful Self-Talk

Negative self-talk is the critical inner dialogue that we engage in when we doubt our abilities, question our worth, or criticize our actions. This harmful self-talk often stems from past experiences, societal pressures, or deep-seated insecurities. It can be a significant barrier to personal growth and happiness.

Have you ever caught yourself thinking, "I'm not smart enough," or "I'll never succeed"? These thoughts can feel automatic, almost like they're part of our daily routine. But what if we could interrupt this pattern and replace it with something positive? How would that transform our lives?

The Impact of Critical Inner Dialogue

Engaging in negative self-talk can have severe consequences for our mental and emotional well-being. It can lead to decreased self-esteem, increased anxiety, and a general sense of hopelessness. Over time, this critical inner dialogue can erode our confidence and prevent us from pursuing our goals.

Think about a recent time when you felt discouraged by your own thoughts. How did it affect your mood and actions? Likely, it made you feel less capable and more hesitant to take on new challenges. Imagine if, instead of tearing yourself down, you built yourself up with encouraging words. How much more motivated and confident would you feel?

Positive Affirmations

Positive affirmations are powerful statements that can help shift your mindset from negative to positive. By regularly practicing positive affirmations, you can cultivate a more supportive inner dialogue and enhance your overall well-being. Here are some techniques to help you incorporate positive affirmations into your daily routine:

1. **Identify Negative Thoughts**: Start by becoming aware of your negative self-talk. Pay attention to the critical

thoughts that pop up throughout your day. Write them down to better understand their frequency and content.

2. **Challenge Negative Thoughts**: Question the validity of your negative thoughts. Are they based on facts or assumptions? Replace them with positive, empowering statements. For example, if you think, "I can't do this," replace it with, "I am capable and can learn new things."

3. **Create Personalized Affirmations**: Develop affirmations that resonate with you and address your specific needs and goals. For instance, if you struggle with self-worth, an affirmation might be, "I am valuable and deserving of love and respect."

4. **Repeat Affirmations Daily**: Set aside time each day to repeat your affirmations. You can do this in front of a mirror, during your morning routine, or before going to bed. Consistency is key to reinforcing positive beliefs.

5. **Visualize Success**: Pair your affirmations with visualization. Picture yourself succeeding and embodying the qualities you affirm. This can enhance the effectiveness of your affirmations.

6. **Surround Yourself with Positivity**: Create an environment that supports your positive mindset. Surround yourself with uplifting people, read inspiring books, and fill your space with positive reminders, like sticky notes with affirmations.

Why Let Go of Negative Self-Talk?

Letting go of negative self-talk can lead to a more positive, fulfilling life. By replacing critical thoughts with supportive affirmations, you can boost your self-esteem, reduce anxiety, and increase your motivation. Cultivating a positive inner dialogue empowers you to pursue your goals and embrace new opportunities with confidence.

Imagine waking up each day feeling encouraged and capable. How would that change your approach to challenges and your overall outlook on life?

Practical Steps for Change

To effectively let go of negative self-talk, consistent effort and self-reflection are essential. Here are some practical steps to guide you:

1. **Daily Reflection**: Spend a few minutes each day reflecting on your thoughts. Identify any negative patterns and consciously replace them with positive affirmations.
2. **Affirmation Journal**: Keep a journal to document your affirmations and track your progress. Write down your affirmations daily and note any positive changes in your mindset and behavior.
3. **Mindfulness Practice**: Practice mindfulness to stay present and aware of your thoughts. Mindfulness techniques, such as meditation and deep breathing, can help you recognize and address negative self-talk.
4. **Support System**: Share your journey with a trusted friend or mentor. They can provide encouragement and hold you accountable as you work to cultivate a positive mindset.
5. **Celebrate Progress**: Acknowledge and celebrate your progress, no matter how small. Recognizing your efforts reinforces positive behavior and keeps you motivated.

Questions for Reflection

1. What negative thoughts do you frequently tell yourself?
2. How does negative self-talk impact your daily life and goals?
3. What positive affirmations can you create to counteract these negative thoughts?
4. How can incorporating positive affirmations into your routine improve your mindset?
5. Who can you rely on for support and encouragement as you work to change your inner dialogue?

Practical Exercise

Choose one negative thought you often have and write it down. Then, create a positive affirmation to counteract this thought. For example, if your negative thought is, "I'm not good enough," your positive affirmation could be, "I am capable and worthy." Repeat this affirmation to yourself every morning and night for one week. At the end of the week, reflect on how this practice has affected your mindset and any changes you've noticed.

Letting go of negative self-talk and embracing positive affirmations can transform your life. By cultivating a supportive inner dialogue, you empower yourself to achieve your goals and live with greater confidence and joy. Remember, the words you say to yourself matter. Choose to speak to yourself with kindness and encouragement, and watch as your mindset and life begin to change for the better.

Chapter 9: Letting Go of Perfectionism

Embrace Your Efforts and Progress Instead of Striving for Perfection

Sophia was always the top student in her class. She graduated with honors, secured a high-paying job, and quickly climbed the corporate ladder. But her success came at a cost. Sophia's relentless pursuit of perfection left her feeling exhausted and anxious. She spent countless hours reworking reports, obsessing over minor details, and fearing that any mistake would undermine her credibility. Despite her achievements, she never felt satisfied; there was always something more she could have done better.

One evening, after missing yet another family dinner due to work, Sophia's younger sister, Mia, confronted her. "Sophia, you're amazing just the way you are. You don't have to be perfect to be loved or respected." This heartfelt message struck a chord with Sophia. She realized that her perfectionism was not only harming her health but also her relationships and overall happiness. Determined to make a change, Sophia began her journey toward embracing imperfection and valuing her efforts and progress.

Perfectionism Problems

Perfectionism is the relentless pursuit of flawlessness and setting excessively high standards for oneself. While striving for excellence can be motivating, perfectionism is counterproductive. It creates unrealistic expectations and an inability to accept anything less than perfect. This mindset often leads to chronic stress, procrastination, and a fear of failure.

Have you ever felt paralyzed by the need to make something perfect, to the point where you delayed starting or completing it? This is a common struggle for perfectionists. But what if we could shift our focus from achieving perfection to appreciating progress? How much more fulfilling would our efforts become?

Why Striving for Perfection Is Counterproductive

Striving for perfection is counterproductive because it sets an unattainable standard. Perfection is an illusion; no matter how hard we try, there will always be room for improvement. This constant pursuit can lead to burnout, decreased productivity, and a lack of satisfaction in our achievements. Additionally, perfectionism can hinder creativity and innovation, as the fear of making mistakes stifles risk-taking and experimentation.

Think about a recent project or task where you aimed for perfection. How did it affect your experience and outcome? Likely, it created unnecessary stress and possibly delayed your progress. Now imagine approaching the same task with a focus on doing your best and learning from the process. How would that change your experience?

Embracing Imperfection

Embracing imperfection involves recognizing that mistakes and flaws are part of the human experience. It means valuing effort and progress over unattainable standards. Here are some strategies to help you embrace imperfection:

1. **Set Realistic Goals**: Establish achievable goals that focus on progress rather than perfection. Break larger tasks into smaller, manageable steps to reduce overwhelm.
2. **Practice Self-Compassion**: Treat yourself with the same kindness and understanding you would offer a friend. Acknowledge your efforts and remind yourself that it's okay to make mistakes.
3. **Celebrate Progress**: Take time to celebrate your achievements, no matter how small. Recognize the value in the journey and the lessons learned along the way.
4. **Shift Your Perspective**: Reframe mistakes as opportunities for growth and learning. Understand that imperfection is a natural part of the process and can lead to valuable insights.
5. **Limit Comparison**: Avoid comparing yourself to others. Everyone has their own unique strengths and weaknesses. Focus on your personal growth and accomplishments.
6. **Mindfulness Practice**: Practice mindfulness to stay present and reduce anxiety about future outcomes. Mindfulness techniques, such as meditation and deep breathing, can help you stay grounded and appreciative of your current efforts.

Why Let Go of Perfectionism?

Letting go of perfectionism allows you to live a more balanced, fulfilling life. By embracing imperfection, you can reduce stress, enhance your well-being, and foster a more positive mindset. It enables you to appreciate your efforts, celebrate progress, and learn from your experiences without the burden of unrealistic expectations.

Imagine the freedom of approaching tasks and projects with a focus on doing your best rather than being perfect. How much more enjoyable and meaningful would your work and life become?

Practical Steps for Change

To effectively let go of perfectionism, consistent effort and self-reflection are essential. Here are some practical steps to guide you:

1. **Daily Reflection**: Spend a few minutes each day reflecting on your efforts and progress. Identify areas where you may have been too hard on yourself and practice self-compassion.
2. **Set Achievable Goals**: Break your goals into smaller, manageable steps. Focus on making steady progress rather than achieving perfection.
3. **Celebrate Small Wins**: Acknowledge and celebrate your accomplishments, no matter how minor they may seem. Recognize the value in each step forward.
4. **Mindfulness Practice**: Incorporate mindfulness exercises into your daily routine to help you stay present and reduce anxiety about imperfections.
5. **Positive Affirmations**: Use positive affirmations to reinforce a growth mindset. Statements like "I am doing my best and that is enough" can help shift your focus from perfection to progress.

Questions for Reflection

1. In what areas of your life do you find yourself striving for

perfection?

2. How has the pursuit of perfection affected your stress levels and overall well-being?

3. What steps can you take to set more realistic, achievable goals?

4. How can you practice self-compassion and celebrate your progress?

5. Who can you share your journey with for support and encouragement as you embrace imperfection?

Practical Exercise

Choose a current project or task that you have been working on. Write down your initial goals and expectations for this project. Then, reassess these goals and adjust them to be more realistic and achievable. Focus on the progress you have made so far and identify at least three positive outcomes or lessons learned. Reflect on how this shift in perspective makes you feel and on any changes in your approach to the task.

Letting go of perfectionism is a journey toward greater self-acceptance and fulfillment. By embracing imperfection, you allow yourself to grow, learn, and appreciate the beauty of progress. Remember, perfection is an illusion, but progress is real and valuable. Celebrate your efforts and enjoy the journey, knowing that you are enough just as you are.

Chapter 10: Letting Go of Toxic Relationships

Distance Yourself from Toxicity and Nurture Positive Relationships

Lena had always been a compassionate and supportive friend. However, her relationship with her college friend, Maya, had become increasingly draining. Maya constantly criticized Lena, belittled her achievements, and often manipulated her into doing things she didn't want to do. Despite feeling unhappy and unvalued, Lena found it difficult to distance herself from Maya because of their long history.

One day, Lena confided in her colleague, Ben, about the situation. Ben listened attentively and then shared his own experience of ending a toxic friendship. "It's tough, but sometimes you have to prioritize your well-being," he said. His words resonated with Lena, and she realized it was time to reassess her relationship with Maya and make a change for her own mental health.

Identifying Toxicity

Toxic relationships can be challenging to identify, especially when they involve people we've known for a long time. These relationships are characterized by behaviors that are emotionally damaging and detrimental to our well-being. Here are some signs of unhealthy relationships:

1. **Constant Criticism**: A toxic person frequently criticizes or belittles you, undermining your self-esteem.
2. **Manipulation**: They manipulate you into doing things against your will, often using guilt or coercion.
3. **Lack of Support**: They are unsupportive of your goals and achievements, often dismissing or downplaying your successes.
4. **Emotional Drain**: Interacting with them leaves you feeling emotionally exhausted and drained.
5. **Control**: They seek to control aspects of your life, from your decisions to your actions and even your thoughts.
6. **Blame and Guilt**: They constantly blame you for problems and make you feel guilty for their actions or emotions.

Have you ever felt relieved after avoiding or leaving an interaction with someone? This could be a sign of a toxic relationship. But what if you could replace these draining interactions with positive, uplifting connections? How would that transform your emotional health?

Why Toxic Relationships Harm Us

Toxic relationships can severely impact our mental, emotional, and even physical health. They can lead to increased stress, anxiety, and a loss of self-esteem. Over time, these relationships can hinder our personal growth and happiness, leaving us feeling stuck and powerless.

Think about a time when a toxic relationship affected your well-being. How did it influence your mood, energy levels, and outlook on life? Imagine freeing yourself from this negativity and surrounding yourself with supportive, positive people. How much more fulfilling and joyful would your life be?

Building Healthy Connections

Letting go of toxic relationships is crucial for your well-being and personal growth. Here are some strategies to help you distance yourself from toxicity and nurture positive relationships:

1. **Identify Toxic Relationships**: Acknowledge and accept that certain relationships in your life may be toxic. This is the first step towards change.
2. **Set Boundaries**: Establish clear boundaries with toxic individuals. Communicate your limits and stick to them, even if it feels uncomfortable at first.
3. **Limit Interaction**: Gradually reduce the time you spend with toxic people. This might involve saying no to invitations or finding reasons to cut interactions short.
4. **Seek Support**: Share your experiences with trusted friends, family, or a therapist. They can provide valuable advice and emotional support.
5. **Focus on Positive Relationships**: Invest time and energy in relationships that uplift and support you. Surround yourself with people who genuinely care about your well-being.
6. **Practice Self-Care**: Prioritize self-care activities that nourish your mind and body. This will help you build resilience and cope with the stress of distancing yourself from toxic individuals.

Why Let Go of Toxic Relationships?

Letting go of toxic relationships allows you to reclaim your emotional health and create space for positive, supportive connections. By distancing yourself from negativity, you can focus on nurturing relationships that enhance your happiness and well-being.

Imagine how liberating it would be to no longer feel drained or anxious after spending time with someone. What new possibilities and positive experiences could you embrace with healthier relationships?

Practical Steps for Change

To effectively let go of toxic relationships, consistent effort and self-reflection are essential. Here are some practical steps to guide you:

1. **Daily Reflection**: Spend a few minutes each day reflecting on your interactions and how they make you feel. Identify any patterns of toxicity.
2. **Set Clear Boundaries**: Write down specific boundaries you need to establish with toxic individuals. Practice communicating these boundaries clearly and assertively.
3. **Gradual Distance**: Develop a plan to gradually reduce contact with toxic people. Start with small steps, such as limiting phone calls or social interactions.
4. **Seek Positive Influences**: Actively seek out and spend time with people who make you feel valued and supported. Join clubs, groups, or communities where you can meet like-minded individuals.
5. **Self-Care Routine**: Establish a self-care routine that includes activities you enjoy and that help you relax. This can be anything from reading and exercising to meditation

and creative hobbies.

Questions for Reflection

1. Which relationships in your life feel emotionally draining or harmful?
2. How do these toxic relationships impact your mental and emotional well-being?
3. What boundaries can you set to protect yourself from toxicity?
4. How can you start nurturing positive relationships in your life?
5. Who can you rely on for support as you distance yourself from toxic individuals?

Practical Exercise

Choose one toxic relationship in your life that you want to address. Write down the behaviors and interactions that make this relationship toxic. Next, outline specific boundaries you need to set to protect yourself. Plan how you will communicate these boundaries and start gradually reducing your contact with this person. Reflect on how these changes impact your well-being and document your progress.

Letting go of toxic relationships is a powerful step towards emotional freedom and personal growth. By creating boundaries and surrounding yourself with positive influences, you can build healthier, more fulfilling connections. Remember, you deserve relationships that uplift and support you. Take the courage to distance yourself from toxicity and embrace the joy of nurturing positive relationships.

Chapter 11: Letting Go of Comparisons

Appreciate Your Unique Journey Instead of Comparing Yourself to Others

Jake was a talented graphic designer who loved his work. However, he couldn't help but compare his progress to that of his peers. He spent hours scrolling through social media, looking at the impressive portfolios and achievements of other designers. Each time, he felt a pang of inadequacy. "Why am I not as successful?" he wondered. This constant comparison drained his motivation and happiness, making him doubt his own abilities.

One day, Jake attended a workshop led by a renowned designer. During a Q&A session, Jake asked how the designer stayed motivated without comparing himself to others. The designer's response was simple yet profound: "Focus on your own growth and the unique value you bring. Everyone's journey is different." Inspired by this advice, Jake decided to shift his focus from comparing himself to appreciating his own progress and talents.

The Comparison Trap

Comparing ourselves to others is a natural but often harmful habit. It involves measuring our achievements, appearance, or circumstances against those of others, usually based on incomplete or skewed information. This habit can undermine our happiness and self-esteem, leading to feelings of inadequacy and dissatisfaction.

Have you ever felt less accomplished or attractive after seeing someone else's success or appearance on social media? This is the comparison trap at work. But what if we could break free from this cycle and focus on our own unique journey? How much more content and confident would we feel?

How Comparing Yourself to Others Undermines Your Happiness

Constantly comparing yourself to others can erode your self-esteem and diminish your happiness. It fosters a mindset of scarcity and competition, where you feel there's not enough success or happiness to go around. This can lead to:

1. **Insecurity**: Believing others are better can make you doubt your own worth and abilities.
2. **Envy**: Wishing for what others have can breed resentment and unhappiness.
3. **Stagnation**: Focusing on others' achievements can distract you from your own goals and progress.
4. **Stress and Anxiety**: Constant comparison can create unnecessary pressure to meet unrealistic standards.

Think about a recent time when you compared yourself to someone else. How did it make you feel? Likely, it left you feeling inadequate or envious. Now imagine if you could channel that energy into appreciating your own journey and achievements. How would that change your outlook?

Focusing on Your Path

Focusing on your own path involves appreciating your unique journey and recognizing your own progress and achievements. Here are some tips to help you shift your focus:

1. **Set Personal Goals**: Define what success means to you based on your values and aspirations, not others'. Create specific, achievable goals that align with your vision.
2. **Celebrate Your Achievements**: Regularly acknowledge and celebrate your accomplishments, no matter how small. Keep a journal to track your progress and milestones.
3. **Limit Social Media Use**: Reduce the time you spend on social media, where comparisons are most likely to occur. Use that time to invest in your hobbies, goals, and personal growth.
4. **Practice Gratitude**: Cultivate gratitude by regularly listing things you appreciate about your life and achievements. This shifts your focus from what you lack to what you have.
5. **Surround Yourself with Supportive People**: Build a network of friends and mentors who support and encourage you. Positive relationships can help reinforce your self-worth and keep you motivated.
6. **Focus on Growth, Not Perfection**: Embrace a growth mindset, where you view challenges and setbacks as opportunities to learn and improve, rather than as failures.

Why Let Go of Comparisons?

Letting go of comparisons allows you to focus on your own growth and happiness. It frees you from the constant pressure to measure up to others and helps you appreciate your unique journey. By valuing your progress and achievements, you can build confidence and find greater satisfaction in your life.

Imagine living each day with a sense of fulfillment and contentment, free from the burden of comparison. How much more joyful and motivated would you be?

Practical Steps for Change

To effectively let go of comparisons, consistent effort and self-reflection are essential. Here are some practical steps to guide you:

1. **Daily Reflection**: Spend a few minutes each day reflecting on your achievements and progress. Identify moments when you felt proud of yourself.
2. **Personal Milestones**: Create a list of personal milestones and goals. Focus on achieving these rather than comparing yourself to others.
3. **Gratitude Practice**: Start a gratitude journal where you list three things you are grateful for each day. This can help shift your focus from what you lack to what you have.
4. **Mindfulness Practice**: Practice mindfulness to stay present and reduce the urge to compare yourself to others. Techniques like meditation and deep breathing can help you stay grounded.
5. **Positive Affirmations**: Use positive affirmations to reinforce your self-worth. Statements like "I am proud of my progress" can help shift your mindset.

Questions for Reflection

1. In what areas of your life do you find yourself most often comparing to others?

2. How does comparing yourself to others affect your happiness and self-esteem?
3. What personal goals can you set to focus on your own journey?
4. How can you practice gratitude and celebrate your achievements?
5. Who can you rely on for support as you work to stop comparing yourself to others?

Practical Exercise

Choose a recent achievement, no matter how small, and write about it in detail. Describe what you did, how you felt, and why it was significant to you. Reflect on what this achievement says about your unique strengths and progress. Repeat this exercise regularly to reinforce your appreciation for your own journey.

Letting go of comparisons is a powerful step towards greater self-acceptance and happiness. By focusing on your own path and celebrating your progress, you can build a more fulfilling and joyful life. Remember, your journey is unique and valuable. Embrace it, and find contentment in your own achievements.

Chapter 12: Letting Go of Unhealthy Lifestyle Habits

Replace Harmful Habits with Healthy Practices for a Better Life

Tom always had a busy schedule. Between work, social commitments, and family obligations, he often found himself resorting to fast food and skipping his workouts. Late nights were spent binge-watching TV shows, and weekends were filled with unhealthy indulgences. Over time, Tom noticed that he felt constantly tired, gained weight, and struggled with stress and low energy. His unhealthy habits were taking a toll on his overall well-being.

One evening, after a particularly exhausting day, Tom's friend Lisa, a fitness enthusiast, visited him. Seeing Tom's state, Lisa shared her own journey of overcoming unhealthy habits. She encouraged Tom to start small and make gradual changes. Inspired by Lisa's transformation, Tom decided it was time to recognize and replace his unhealthy lifestyle habits with healthier ones.

Recognizing Bad Habits

Unhealthy lifestyle habits can be deeply ingrained and challenging to identify. They often develop over time and become part of our daily routine. Here are some common unhealthy habits that can harm your health:

1. **Poor Diet**: Consuming excessive amounts of junk food, sugary snacks, and processed foods.
2. **Lack of Exercise**: Leading a sedentary lifestyle with minimal physical activity.
3. **Inadequate Sleep**: Not getting enough quality sleep or having an irregular sleep schedule.
4. **Excessive Screen Time**: Spending too much time on electronic devices, leading to reduced physical activity and poor posture.
5. **Chronic Stress**: Not managing stress effectively, leading to mental and physical health issues.
6. **Substance Abuse**: Overindulging in alcohol, smoking, or using recreational drugs.

Have you ever noticed how a single bad habit can spiral into a series of unhealthy behaviors? Recognizing these habits is the first step towards making positive changes. But what if you could replace these harmful habits with ones that enhance your well-being? How would that improve your life?

Why Bad Habits Harm Your Health

Unhealthy habits can have a significant negative impact on your physical, mental, and emotional well-being. They can lead to chronic health conditions, increased stress, and a reduced quality of life. Over time, these habits can become harder to break, trapping you in a cycle of poor health and low energy.

Think about a habit you know is unhealthy. How does it affect your daily life and overall well-being? Now imagine replacing that habit with a healthier one. How would that change your energy levels, mood, and health?

Adopting Healthy Practices

Replacing unhealthy habits with healthier ones requires commitment and consistency. Here are some steps to help you make the transition:

1. **Identify Unhealthy Habits**: Make a list of your current habits that negatively impact your health. Be honest with yourself about the areas that need improvement.

2. **Set Specific Goals**: Define clear, achievable goals for each unhealthy habit you want to change. For example, aim to replace sugary snacks with fruits or commit to a 30-minute daily walk.

3. **Start Small**: Begin with small, manageable changes. Gradual adjustments are more sustainable and less overwhelming than drastic changes.

4. **Create a Plan**: Develop a plan for how you will replace unhealthy habits with healthy ones. This might include meal planning, scheduling exercise, or setting a bedtime routine.

5. **Track Progress**: Keep a journal to monitor your progress. Note the changes you make, how they affect your well-being, and any challenges you encounter.

6. **Seek Support**: Share your goals with friends, family, or a support group. Having accountability partners can motivate you and provide encouragement.

7. **Reward Yourself**: Celebrate your successes, no matter how small. Rewards can help reinforce positive behavior and keep you motivated.

Why Let Go of Unhealthy Habits?

Letting go of unhealthy habits and adopting healthier ones can lead to a more vibrant, energetic, and fulfilling life. By making positive changes, you can improve your physical health, boost your mental well-being, and enhance your overall quality of life.

Imagine waking up each day feeling refreshed, energized, and motivated. How much more could you accomplish and enjoy life with a healthier lifestyle?

Practical Steps for Change

To effectively let go of unhealthy habits, consistent effort and self-reflection are essential. Here are some practical steps to guide you:

1. **Daily Reflection**: Spend a few minutes each day reflecting on your habits and their impact on your health. Identify areas for improvement and plan your next steps.
2. **Set Achievable Goals**: Break your goals into smaller, manageable steps. Focus on making steady progress rather than seeking perfection.
3. **Create a Routine**: Establish a daily routine that incorporates healthy habits. Consistency is key to forming new, positive behaviors.
4. **Mindfulness Practice**: Practice mindfulness to stay present and make conscious choices about your habits. Techniques like meditation and deep breathing can help you stay focused.
5. **Positive Affirmations**: Use positive affirmations to reinforce your commitment to a healthy lifestyle. Statements like "I choose healthy habits that nourish my body and mind" can help motivate you.

Questions for Reflection

1. What unhealthy habits do you currently have that impact your well-being?
2. How do these habits affect your physical, mental, and emotional health?
3. What specific goals can you set to replace these unhealthy habits with healthy ones?
4. How can you create a plan to incorporate healthy practices into your daily routine?
5. Who can you rely on for support and accountability as you work to change your habits?

Practical Exercise

Choose one unhealthy habit you want to change. Write down why you want to change it and how it affects your life. Then, create a step-by-step plan to replace this habit with a healthier one. For example, if you want to reduce your screen time before bed, set a goal to read a book or meditate for 30 minutes instead. Track your progress over the next two weeks and reflect on how this change impacts your well-being.

Letting go of unhealthy lifestyle habits and embracing healthier practices is a journey toward a better quality of life. By making mindful choices and staying committed to your goals, you can transform your health and well-being. Remember, each small step forward is progress. Celebrate your efforts and enjoy the benefits of a healthier, more vibrant life.

Chapter 13: Letting Go of Chronic Worry

Manage Worry and Focus on Living in the Present

Linda was a successful project manager, known for her meticulous attention to detail and strong work ethic. However, her professional success came with a hidden burden: chronic worry. Linda is constantly worried about meeting deadlines, potential mistakes, and even things beyond her control, like her company's financial health. This constant state of worry seeped into her personal life, causing sleepless nights, tension headaches, and strained relationships.

One day, after a particularly stressful week, Linda's close friend, Jason, suggested she try mindfulness meditation to manage her anxiety. Jason shared how practicing mindfulness had helped him let go of his own worries and live more fully in the present. Intrigued and desperate for relief, Linda decided to give it a try. Over time, she learned to manage her worries and focus on the present, finding a new sense of peace and balance.

Worry Woes

Chronic worry is the excessive and uncontrollable concern about potential problems and uncertainties in life. It can consume your thoughts, making it difficult to focus on the present and enjoy life. Chronic worry often stems from a desire to control outcomes and avoid potential negative events, but ironically, it usually leads to increased stress and anxiety.

Have you ever found yourself lost in a cycle of "what if" thoughts, unable to enjoy the moment because you're preoccupied with future uncertainties? This is the nature of chronic worry. But what if you could break free from this cycle and live more fully in the present? How much more peaceful and enjoyable would your life be?

How Constant Worrying Affects Your Well-Being

Constant worrying can have severe impacts on your mental, emotional, and physical health. It can lead to:

1. **Increased Stress and Anxiety**: Chronic worry keeps your body in a constant state of stress, leading to anxiety disorders.
2. **Sleep Disturbances**: Worrying can cause insomnia or poor sleep quality, leaving you exhausted and less able to cope with daily challenges.
3. **Physical Health Issues**: Prolonged stress from worry can lead to headaches, digestive problems, and a weakened immune system.
4. **Emotional Strain**: Worrying can drain your emotional energy, making it hard to experience joy and leading to feelings of hopelessness.

Think about a recent situation where worry dominated your thoughts. How did it affect your mood, energy, and interactions with others? Now imagine being able to let go of these worries and live in the present moment. How would that change your experience?

Living in the Present

Living in the present involves focusing on the current moment rather than being preoccupied with past regrets or future uncertainties. Here are some techniques to help you manage worry and stay present:

1. **Mindfulness Meditation**: Practice mindfulness meditation to train your mind to focus on the present. This can help reduce anxiety and improve your overall sense of well-being.

2. **Deep Breathing Exercises**: Use deep breathing exercises to calm your mind and body when you start to feel overwhelmed by worry. This can help you regain focus and clarity.

3. **Grounding Techniques**: Engage in grounding techniques, such as paying attention to your five senses or counting backward from 100, to bring your attention back to the present.

4. **Positive Affirmations**: Use positive affirmations to counteract negative thoughts and worries. Affirmations like "I am in control of my thoughts and choose to focus on the present" can be empowering.

5. **Limit Worry Time**: Allocate a specific time each day for worrying. When worries arise outside of this time, remind yourself that you have set aside time to address them later.

6. **Engage in Present Activities**: Participate in activities that require your full attention, such as exercising, cooking, or hobbies. This can help shift your focus from worries to the present moment.

Why Let Go of Chronic Worry?

Letting go of chronic worry allows you to live a more peaceful and fulfilling life. By managing your worries and focusing on the present, you can reduce stress, improve your mental and physical health, and enjoy each moment more fully.

Imagine waking up each day with a clear mind, free from the constant burden of worry. How much more enjoyable and productive would your days be?

Practical Steps for Change

To effectively let go of chronic worry, consistent effort and self-reflection are essential. Here are some practical steps to guide you:

1. **Daily Reflection**: Spend a few minutes each day reflecting on your worries and their impact on your well-being. Identify patterns and triggers.
2. **Mindfulness Practice**: Incorporate mindfulness exercises into your daily routine to help you stay present and reduce anxiety.
3. **Worry Journal**: Keep a worry journal to document your worries and track their frequency and intensity. This can help you identify and address underlying issues.
4. **Positive Affirmations**: Use positive affirmations daily to reinforce a calm and focused mindset.
5. **Engage in Present Activities**: Dedicate time each day to activities that require your full attention and bring you joy.

Questions for Reflection

1. What are the most common worries that occupy your mind?

2. How does chronic worrying affect your daily life and well-being?
3. What techniques can you use to manage your worries and focus on the present?
4. How would living more in the present change your outlook on life?
5. Who can you rely on for support as you work to let go of chronic worry?

Practical Exercise

Choose a specific time each day to practice mindfulness meditation for at least 10 minutes. During this time, focus on your breath and gently bring your attention back whenever your mind starts to wander. After your meditation session, write down any worries that came up and reflect on how the practice made you feel. Repeat this exercise daily for two weeks and observe any changes in your anxiety levels and ability to stay present.

Letting go of chronic worry and learning to live in the present is a journey toward greater peace and fulfillment. By practicing mindfulness and focusing on the here and now, you can reduce stress and enhance your quality of life. Remember, each moment is an opportunity to experience joy and contentment. Embrace it, and let go of the worries that hold you back.

Chapter 14: Letting Go of Regrets

Release Regrets and Live More Fully

Michael had always been a thoughtful person, often reflecting on past decisions and their outcomes. However, this habit sometimes turned into dwelling on missed opportunities and mistakes. He regretted not pursuing his passion for music, the time he lost touch with an old friend, and the career choices he felt were safe but unfulfilling. These regrets weighed heavily on him, making it hard to enjoy his present life and look forward to the future.

One evening, Michael met his former mentor, Emily, at a reunion event. Emily had faced her own set of regrets but seemed genuinely content and at peace. Curious, Michael asked her how she had moved past her regrets. Emily shared how she embraced forgiveness, learned from her experiences, and focused on living fully in the present. Inspired by Emily's approach, Michael decided it was time to let go of his regrets and make the most of his life.

The Burden of Regret

Regret is a powerful emotion that arises from reflecting on past actions, decisions, or missed opportunities with a sense of loss or disappointment. It can be a heavy burden, holding you back from experiencing joy and fulfillment in the present. Regrets can manifest in various forms, such as:

1. **Missed Opportunities**: Wishing you had taken a different path or seized a chance.
2. **Mistakes Made**: Dwelling on actions you wish you hadn't taken or things you wish you had done differently.
3. **Unresolved Relationships**: Feeling remorse over relationships that ended poorly or were neglected.

Have you ever found yourself replaying past events in your mind, wishing you could go back and change them? This constant focus on what might have been can prevent you from appreciating the present and moving forward. But what if you could release these regrets and embrace your current life fully? How much lighter and more joyful would you feel?

Understanding How Regrets Hold You Back

Living with regret can have a significant impact on your mental and emotional well-being. It can lead to:

1. **Emotional Pain**: Regrets often come with feelings of sadness, guilt, and self-blame.
2. **Stagnation**: Constantly focusing on the past can keep you from taking action and making positive changes in your life.
3. **Reduced Self-Esteem**: Regret can make you question your worth and abilities, diminishing your confidence.
4. **Missed Present Opportunities**: Being preoccupied with past regrets can cause you to overlook opportunities and experiences in the present.

Think about a regret that you frequently revisit. How does it make you feel, and how does it affect your daily life? Imagine being free from this burden, focusing instead on what you can do now to create a fulfilling life.

Moving Forward

Releasing regrets and moving forward involves acknowledging your feelings, learning from your experiences, and focusing on the present. Here are some steps to help you let go of regrets and live more fully:

1. **Acknowledge Your Regrets**: Identify and accept your regrets. Write them down to understand their impact on your life.
2. **Forgive Yourself**: Practice self-compassion and forgive yourself for past mistakes and missed opportunities. Remember that everyone makes mistakes, and it's part of being human.
3. **Learn from the Past**: Reflect on what you can learn from your regrets. Use these insights to make better decisions and avoid repeating the same patterns.
4. **Set New Goals**: Focus on setting new, achievable goals that align with your values and aspirations. This can help you redirect your energy toward positive actions.
5. **Practice Mindfulness**: Engage in mindfulness practices to stay present and reduce the tendency to dwell on the past. Techniques like meditation and deep breathing can help.
6. **Seek Support**: Talk to trusted friends, family, or a therapist about your regrets. Sharing your feelings can provide relief and new perspectives.

Why Let Go of Regrets?

Letting go of regrets allows you to reclaim your emotional freedom and focus on creating a fulfilling future. By releasing the weight of past mistakes and missed opportunities, you can experience greater joy, peace, and motivation.

Imagine living each day with a sense of possibility and contentment, free from the shadows of the past. How would this change your approach to life and your overall happiness?

Practical Steps for Change

To effectively let go of regrets, consistent effort and self-reflection are essential. Here are some practical steps to guide you:

1. **Daily Reflection**: Spend a few minutes each day reflecting on your progress in letting go of regrets. Acknowledge your efforts and any positive changes you notice.
2. **Mindfulness Practice**: Incorporate mindfulness exercises into your daily routine to help you stay present and reduce dwelling on the past.
3. **Gratitude Journal**: Keep a gratitude journal to focus on the positive aspects of your life. List three things you are grateful for each day to shift your perspective from regret to appreciation.
4. **Positive Affirmations**: Use positive affirmations to reinforce your commitment to living fully in the present. Statements like "I release my regrets and embrace the opportunities of today" can be empowering.
5. **Engage in New Experiences**: Actively seek out new experiences and opportunities that align with your values and interests. This can help you create positive memories and

reduce the focus on past regrets.

Questions for Reflection

1. What regrets do you frequently revisit, and how do they affect your well-being?
2. How can you practice self-forgiveness and compassion to release these regrets?
3. What lessons can you learn from your past experiences that can guide your future decisions?
4. How can mindfulness and gratitude practices help you stay present and reduce regret?
5. Who can you talk to for support and encouragement as you work to let go of your regrets?

Practical Exercise

Choose one regret that you frequently think about. Write a letter to yourself describing the regret, how it has affected you, and what you have learned from it. Then, write a paragraph forgiving yourself for this regret and committing to focus on the present. Read this letter aloud to yourself, then store it in a safe place or symbolically let it go by tearing it up or burning it. Reflect on how this exercise makes you feel and any changes in your mindset.

Letting go of regrets and focusing on the present is a powerful step towards greater peace and fulfillment. By embracing your past experiences and using them to guide your future, you can create a more joyful and meaningful life. Remember, each day is an opportunity to live fully and make the most of the present moment. Embrace it, and let go of the regrets that hold you back.

Chapter 15: Letting Go of Resistance to Change

Nina had always enjoyed a predictable routine. She liked knowing what to expect each day, from her morning coffee to her evening walk. However, when her company announced a major restructuring that required her to take on new responsibilities and learn new skills, Nina felt overwhelmed and anxious. She resisted the changes, clinging to her old ways and fearing the unknown.

One afternoon, Nina confided in her colleague, Alex, who had recently adapted successfully to a similar change. Alex shared his experience and the strategies he used to embrace the new opportunities. Nina made the decision to alter her perspective and approach the situation as a challenge rather than a threat in response to Alex's upbeat attitude and practical advice.

Change as a Challenge

Fear of the unknown, a loss of control, and comfort with the status quo are common reasons for resistance to change. It's a natural human response to want to maintain stability and predictability in life. However, this resistance can limit personal growth, opportunities, and overall well-being.

Have you ever found yourself resisting a change, even though it might lead to positive outcomes? This resistance often stems from fear and uncertainty. But what if you could see change as an opportunity for growth and new experiences? How would that transform your approach to life?

Why We Resist Change and How It Limits Us

Resisting change can have several negative impacts on our lives, including:

1. **Stagnation**: Clinging to the familiar can prevent personal and professional growth.
2. **Missed Opportunities**: Fear of change can lead to missed chances for new experiences, skills, and relationships.
3. **Increased Stress**: Constant resistance creates stress and anxiety, as fighting against inevitable changes can be exhausting.
4. **Lack of Adaptability**: An inability to adapt to change can hinder success in dynamic environments, both at work and in personal life.

Think about a recent change you resisted. How did it affect your stress levels and overall happiness? Imagine embracing that change and the potential benefits it could bring. How would that change your outlook and experience?

Embracing Change

Embracing change involves shifting your mindset and developing strategies to adapt positively. Here are some tips to help you welcome and adapt to change:

1. **Acknowledge Your Feelings**: Recognize and accept your

emotions about the change. It's okay to feel anxious or uncertain, but acknowledging these feelings is the first step towards managing them.

2. **Stay Informed**: Gather information about the change to understand what it involves and how it will impact you. Knowledge can reduce fear and uncertainty.

3. **Focus on the Positives**: Identify potential benefits and opportunities that the change may bring. Shifting your focus to positive outcomes can help you feel more optimistic.

4. **Set Realistic Goals**: Break down the change into manageable steps and set achievable goals. This can make the process feel less overwhelming and more attainable.

5. **Develop a Support System**: Surround yourself with supportive friends, family, or colleagues who can offer encouragement and advice.

6. **Practice Flexibility**: Cultivate a flexible mindset that allows you to adapt to new situations. Being open to change can make it easier to navigate transitions.

7. **Self-Care**: Take care of your physical and mental well-being during times of change. Regular exercise, healthy eating, and mindfulness practices can help you stay resilient.

Why Let Go of Resistance to Change?

Letting go of resistance to change allows you to embrace new opportunities, foster personal growth, and reduce stress. By viewing change as a challenge rather than a threat, you can approach life with greater adaptability and confidence.

Imagine feeling excited and empowered by changes rather than fearful and resistant. How much more dynamic and fulfilling would your life become?

Practical Steps for Change

To effectively let go of resistance to change, consistent effort and self-reflection are essential. Here are some practical steps to guide you:

1. **Daily Reflection**: Spend a few minutes each day reflecting on recent changes and your reactions to them. Identify any patterns of resistance and areas for improvement.
2. **Mindfulness Practice**: Incorporate mindfulness exercises into your daily routine to help you stay present and manage anxiety about change.
3. **Positive Affirmations**: Use positive affirmations to reinforce your adaptability and openness to change. Statements like "I embrace change and the opportunities it brings" can be empowering.
4. **Action Plan**: Create an action plan for a current or upcoming change. Outline the steps you need to take and set small, achievable goals to guide your progress.
5. **Seek Support**: Engage with a mentor, coach, or support group to share your experiences and gain new perspectives on managing change.

Questions for Reflection

1. What recent changes have you resisted, and why?
2. How has resisting change affected your stress levels and personal growth?
3. What potential benefits can you identify in the changes you face?
4. How can you develop a more flexible mindset to embrace change?

5. Who can you turn to for support and encouragement as you navigate changes?

Practical Exercise

Choose a current or upcoming change in your life. Write down your initial feelings and reactions to this change. Next, list the potential benefits and opportunities it may bring. Create an action plan with specific steps you can take to adapt to the change positively. Reflect on this exercise daily for a week, noting any shifts in your perspective and feelings about the change.

Letting go of resistance to change is a crucial step towards a more adaptable and fulfilling life. By embracing change and viewing it as a challenge, you can reduce stress and open yourself up to new possibilities. Remember, change is an inevitable part of life, and how you respond to it can significantly impact your happiness and success. Embrace the journey and welcome the opportunities that change can bring.

Now WHAT? You May Ask

The Turning Point

So, you've taken a deep breath and decided to let go of various burdens—resentments, fears, unrealistic expectations, and more. You've read through each chapter, nodding in agreement, feeling a spark of hope. But now, standing at this new juncture, you might be wondering, "Now what?"

The Journey Ahead

It's natural to feel a mix of excitement and uncertainty at this point. You've embarked on a journey of self-discovery and transformation. But where do you go from here? How do you ensure that the changes you've started to make become lasting parts of your life? The answer lies in small, consistent steps.

Building Consistency

Change doesn't happen overnight. It requires daily effort and a commitment to your new way of living. Have you ever tried to start a new habit only to give up a few days later? It's a common experience, but the key is persistence. What small steps can you take today to reinforce the positive changes you've begun?

Setting Realistic Goals

One effective strategy is to set realistic, achievable goals. These goals should be specific and manageable. For example, if you've decided to let go of negative self-talk, your goal could be to write down one positive affirmation each morning. Can you imagine how these small actions, over time, can lead to significant improvements in your mindset?

Staying Motivated

Motivation can wane, especially when faced with challenges. What can you do to stay motivated? Surround yourself with supportive people who encourage your growth. Celebrate your progress, no matter how small. Remember, it's not about perfection; it's about progress. How can you remind yourself of this daily?

Reflecting Regularly

Reflection is a powerful tool for sustaining change. Take time each day to reflect on your journey. What have you accomplished? What challenges have you faced, and how did you overcome them? Reflecting helps you stay connected to your goals and reminds you of your resilience. How can you incorporate reflection into your routine?

Embracing Flexibility

Life is unpredictable, and sometimes, despite our best efforts, things don't go as planned. How do you handle setbacks? Embrace flexibility and understand that setbacks are a part of the journey. What matters is how you respond to them. Can you view these moments as opportunities to learn and grow?

Seeking Support

Don't be afraid to seek support when you need it. Whether it's a friend, family member, or professional, having someone to talk to can make a big difference. Have you identified someone in your life who can offer you the support you need?

Celebrating Milestones

As you continue on this path, take time to celebrate your milestones. Each achievement, no matter how small, is a testament to your hard work and dedication. Can you plan small rewards for yourself to acknowledge these successes?

Creating a Vision

Finally, create a vision for your future. What do you want your life to look like in a year, five years, or even ten years? Visualizing your desired future can provide you with direction and motivation. Can you see the person you're becoming and the life you're building?

Moving Forward with Confidence

Standing at this juncture, the question "Now what?" transforms from uncertainty into opportunity. You've done the hard work of letting go of what no longer serves you. Now, it's time to embrace the possibilities that lie ahead. With clear goals, consistent effort, and unwavering support, you are equipped to create a fulfilling and joyful life. So, what's your next step?

Take a moment right now to write down one small action you can take today to move forward. It could be as simple as a positive affirmation, a few minutes of reflection, or reaching out to a supportive friend. Whatever it is, make it specific and doable. This is your journey, and every step you take brings you closer to the life you envision. So, now what? You move forward, with confidence and hope.

Conclusion

A Journey of Transformation

Congratulations on reaching the end of this transformative journey. By diving into each chapter and exploring the steps to let go of various burdens, you have taken significant strides toward a more fulfilling and joyful life. It's been a path of self-discovery, reflection, and positive change, and you should be incredibly proud of the progress you've made.

Thank You for Reading

I want to extend my heartfelt gratitude to you for purchasing and reading this book. Your willingness to invest in yourself and embrace these concepts is truly commendable. I hope the insights and strategies shared have resonated with you and provided you with the tools needed to let go of what no longer serves you.

A Ripple Effect of Positivity

Your journey doesn't end here. Every step you take towards a better life not only benefits you but also those around you. Your newfound positivity, resilience, and strength can inspire others to embark on their own journeys of change and growth. Imagine the ripple effect of positivity you can create simply by living your best life.

Your Voice Matters

If this book has touched your life and helped you in any way, I kindly ask you to share your experience by leaving a review. Your feedback is invaluable—it helps me, as an author, continue to improve and reach more readers. More importantly, your review can guide others who may need to hear these messages. It can provide the encouragement they need to pick up this book and start their own journey toward a better life.

Empower Others

By sharing your thoughts and experiences, you empower others to take that crucial first step. Your review could be the nudge someone needs to begin letting go of their own burdens and embrace a more positive and fulfilling future. Imagine the impact your words can have on someone else's life.

A Final Word

Thank you once again for joining me on this journey. I hope you continue to embrace the changes you've made and keep moving forward with confidence and hope. Remember, each day is an opportunity to live fully and joyfully. Keep reflecting, growing, and celebrating your progress. You are capable of amazing things.

Share Your Story

Please take a moment to leave a review and share your story. Your voice is powerful, and together, we can reach and inspire countless others. Thank you for being a part of this journey and for contributing to a community of growth, positivity, and transformation.

With gratitude and best wishes for your continued journey,
Yakalou

Made in United States
Troutdale, OR
07/15/2024